I0528071

The Grief Committee Minutes

SAINT JULIAN PRESS

POETRY

Praise for *The Grief Committee Minutes*

How the past haunts us, even as life goes on. And how the birds—ah, the birds—match us, tapping and feeding and squabbling and, once in a while, showing us how to fly. Sarah Carey flies in this book—her dead mother on her back, the past in all its complications, yes, but fly she does. The poetry, "the wing //my life careens on to its close." A good read.

—Alice Friman
On the Overnight Train: New and Selected Poems

This remarkable debut resides in a liminal space, striding between natural and spiritual realms. Sarah Carey doesn't miss anything, not the blur of a peregrine wing nor the secrets of an ailing father. In some ways, *The Grief Committee Minutes* is a book-length elegy, mourning the poet's lost family but also the fleetingness of life in general. We don't get to stay in this beautiful, difficult space for long. Instead, "we learn to live, as Atlas did, with the heavens / holding each other, the world." This book teems with life even as it looks death in the eye, never flinching. A wild, wonderful collection of poems.

—Erica Wright
All the Bayou Stories End with Drowned

On the timelessness of grief, Carey's moving debut deftly captures the "end to means to end" by which "we let each other go." With startling clarity, these poems detail multiple articulations of self and home that carry across generations, in which loss is both finite and infinite. Parental loss, the pandemic losses, and aging (loss of self) are imbricated in these poems, asking the reader to consider what is knowable and unknowable about a life and those who are closest to us. In lyrics that are spare and cutting, rangy and lush, this thanatological collection thrills with beauty and its passing, with the ways the past is embedded in the present, and with the lives one attempts to rescue through memory. Its buoyant music dazzles and haunts.

—Chelsea Dingman
Thaw and *I,Divided*

Sarah Carey's luminous new poems reckon with our beautiful and broken world with the intimacy and precision of a writer at her peak. Daughter of a dying mother and a threatened Earth, she grafts truths that root her and her readers in shared history, place—and the strength to rise like the pines and swallow-tails on these pages. "Why rebuild?" Carey asks in an electrifying hurricane poem. This collection holds the answers, and all that is dear.

—Cynthia Barnett
Rain and *The Sound of the Sea*

In her stunning debut, *The Grief Committee Minutes*, Sarah Carey offers a yearning litany of familial love, spirituality, and the inevitable loss and grief that defines the human condition. In each poem, no matter the topic—from horseback riding lessons and hurricanes to dementia and war—the reader can distinguish the angst, the bargaining, and the reckoning with which the poet wrestles. "Like any good flame / I tapered, acquiescing / to my extinction," she writes in "What We Read About Ukraine Makes Us Dream of Burning." But taken as a whole, these accessible, recognizable poems with their soaring imagery, most often viewed through the lens of the natural, northern Florida world, are also about the persistence of faith and the steadfastness of true companions, human and otherwise. Carey's tone is often curious, gentle, and accepting. "No one knows the ways / we let each other go," she writes in "The Beach House Offers an Elegy." But her phrasing is also incisive, perceptive, and quick-witted. In the end, her tight command of language convinces readers that perhaps it is she who controls the world around her rather than the other way around.

—Jen Karetnick
Inheritance with a High Error Rate
Winner of the 2022 Cider Press Book Award

The Grief
Committee Minutes

Sarah Carey

SAINT JULIAN PRESS
HOUSTON

Published by
SAINT JULIAN PRESS, Inc.
2053 Cortlandt, Suite 200
Houston, Texas 77008

www.saintjulianpress.com

COPYRIGHT © 2024
TWO THOUSAND AND TWENTY-FOUR
©Sarah Carey

Paperback ISBN-13: 978-1-955194-37-2
E-Book ISBN: 978-1-955194-38-9
Library of Congress Control Number: 2024940118

Cover Art Credit: *Sandhill Cranes at Paynes Prairie Preserve State Park*
Photo by Stephen L. Tabone. Design by Mary Cecelia.

Author Photo Credit: Adrienne Fletcher

For Chad, Justin, Brady, and Krystal, and for my sisters,
Marylynn, Beth, Joanna, and Jessica

In memory of my mother, Sally Stanback Malloy

CONTENTS

EVIDENCE

I MADE A LIST OF THINGS I HAVE
TO REMEMBER AND A LIST
OF THINGS I WANT TO FORGET,
BUT I SEE THEY ARE THE SAME LIST.
—LINDA PASTAN

The Grief Committee
Minutes

Flyover

The Grief Committee

A black racer who played dead as a vice chair's visibility
in the dollarweed, holding the secret of his life

or hidden in the loropetalum you pruned
each spring as you approached—

he'll be there, as will the secretary chickadees you see each fall
at the feeder, caching thousands of seeds like minutes

in cavities of bark and tree. Don't forget
the sleepy millipedes curled up on the porch—

the ones you swept away, time after time,
yet they crawled back predictably—

an inconvenience, but what would life be
without them, scavenging decay in spaces you'll never go—

under logs, or beneath the damp lawn thatch.
All your precious Labradors will retrieve their leashes,

tethered to you once again. The auditor wolf you feared
sends all his best, regrets. Human ad-hocs

register petitions of forgiveness, a fresh start,
each beating heart and memory preserved

in the meeting minutes. By her muted feathers
you'll discern the young, red-shouldered hawk,

a fixture on your backyard post,
facing the scene of her last kill,

while the grief committee chairs, the cranes,
who see it all, as sandhills do, plan the annual gala—

tables for the lost, our newly bereaved,
in a sky of white cloths, with your mother's silver,

gardenias for a centerpiece. They'll bugle their flock
of mourners for you, setting every place.

Avian Inventory

Nothing on the planet is faster
than the peregrine diving for prey
at speeds where lungs by rights

should burst, but theirs survive—
thanks to a bony bump in the nose
disrupting airflow, says the guide

from a look-out as I squinted hope
but missed the flight, imagine the world's
most widespread raptor, the wing

my life careens on to its close,
as I inventory sightings overlooked—
a flock of kites foraging

in the lowlands, whooping cranes stooping
for grubs on the prairie—
crooked grace, red-faced outlier

among silvery sandhills, where I dreamt the thrill
of being first in my reporting but lived
for rapture others left in logs.

The point is vanishing, an empty sky
where my head spins, full of the missing,
never seen or to be seen again—

until one late May day, black silhouette
against white feather slices my field
of vision, draws my eyes high

above the building corners
and where I'd given up on dancing,
in the span of seconds and eternity,

a single swallow-tail glides.

Space Invaders

My body homes itinerant ghosts—
stretched, like a long story,

shapeshifting as it becomes itself,
bends end to means to end

where I begin, inside my mother,
pushing toward release. Ghosts of gut-

level fear in the forming face,
of afterbirth, shed in the final stage

of delivery. Antsy ghosts, aghast
at the last taste of first blood,

mouth a legacy of maternal ancestors—
a line they know now dies

with me, curved on the floor in balasana.
Mama, mama.

Ghosts of the amnion, breaking.

Proof

"The basic anxiety, the anxiety of a finite being about the threat of non-being, cannot be eliminated. It belongs to existence itself."
—*Paul Tillich*

You have to come to faith on your own, I'd said,
that you could believe anything if you commit to witness.
When the white-tailed doe strolled into our enclave
before the rain, drawn where roots send sugars up,
sweet sweep of green in spring, to what remains
of old growth in a region recently clear cut, I imagined
anthropomorphically, that we were its curiosities.
As if something in us were capable of saving.
I told you, the past is more than a remembering,
a resurrection of guilt, or an endless mourning
for all the answers never given, or come too late
to believe. For what we never asked.
I said, *trust me.* I am one who lies at times, it's true,
but not about what matters. Lies like, no, I didn't see you
when I really did, or yes, it's fine with me
if the only chapels you'll set foot in anymore are woods.
When we saw the doe together, saw it see us watching,
freeze, we sensed its fear of being seen. Of being/
non-being. Out of place, of time. Then we saw it beeline
for the asphalt curling around our cul-de-sac,
the devil it didn't know, and bolt, leap hedges,
trample landscaping to escape, until a pathway opened
to a clearing somehow I knew it would find.
All that's left now is its imprint on my mind.
Then, I said, *now do you believe me?*

It Wasn't a Muscle, a Bone or a Gene
That Made Us Human

but a spark, the scientist said.
Generations from scaled histories—

single cell to comb jelly, fish to amphibian,
bird, primate, mammal, hybrids
in between, I emerge in human form

to hover, neoprened, over pods of rainbow
parrotfish, queen angel, known for the spot
on the head some say resembles a crown—

Amphitrite's here, alongside barracuda,
blue-striped grunt. Electric shapes that flitting

flash intent in hide-and-seek. They constellate,
disperse. Social fish, in shoals parade

a show in wordless code—
dart/dash, flip/flutter, living their best life

while others, solo, seek refuge in rift,
a reef's remarkable decline, in layers

of thermocline. I rise to empty
my mask of salt, then dive
a little deeper, although little could I know the ways

our predecessors held their own,
their range, or what the world looked like to them

before the humans came.

The Brazilian Peppertrees

For years they grew, like conspiracy theories
strangling mangroves, stealing all the light

from the sun we worshipped from our patio
where we faced the dunes we called our dunes,
palming mugs filled with espresso at daybreak.

So much native vegetation, we said when we closed,
when brown rabbits still crossed bushes

full of passionflower, but did not foresee
the dense, orange-berried trees

spreading their canopy of lies. We called them
beautiful, exotic, nesting in our neat
vacation space, while drupe by drupe

they colonized, marauders all those years
we failed to recognize, until one day

returning to the place we called our place,
we stepped outside, surveyed the scene
the way we always did to criticize our views

—we lost the ocean long ago—

saw squirrels race past stump cambiums,
a maw a landscaper had clawed. We knew

the sight was temporary—
birds scatter seeds to form new stands
while we are sleeping, dying, dead—

but for now, for just what's left
of us, for all we still discern,
our faces fill with light.

A Pileated Woodpecker Shares Where to Find God

I live for what the dead give.

Hidden by leaf screens and branches,
I pillage rotting wood. My tribe fought
long for salvation, after the forests' razing,

dug into ragged stumps, felled trunks—
a miracle of wholeness from fragments,
a feast of insects who thrive on decay.

What's left when I leave is for others to say.

Should you see my black wings
and red head knocking wood for nourishment,

you might ask if I believe God is dead,
as Altizer said, that God lived and died
in Christ, that the church lied
about becoming the body—but what Altizer said

was not what most thought he meant,
he really meant in death, life—a spirit

indwelling to drill the dying down,
incarnate carnage, God's passion.

If you ask me, I'm proof he was right.

If you listen to my rat-a-tat melody
echoing my drumming beak, you may hear
an answered prayer of oneness in desire's

shrill tattoo, and the thrumming
of your own wild heart.

Flyover
(for my mother)

It's not the same Miami, I would tell you
—if you could know what I mean—

three hundred and sixty miles from Tallahassee,
at least fifty years since your last trip home,

sixty-five since you married my father,
who was never again driven to visit
the in-laws, your part of the world as cloudy

as a marriage you barely remember.
On approach, a guitar-shaped hotel
either marvel or neon monstrosity shoots toward sky—

imagine its lit strings at night,
highlighting the next-door casino

run by the Seminole, the games,
the many ways we gamble. I stow you
like carry-on, my good-luck chip.

Would show you—if you could know what I mean—
the still canal on my right, as ubiquitous now

as in your childhood, all that talk of drainage
from the swamplands, dredge-and-fill,
a watershed of tears.

Then to my left, a sign
we've entered the reservation

we never made with the future—but tell that
to the egret high-stepping in a marsh,

seeking any edible remnant,
what's left of your Everglades.

It's Common for Alzheimer's Patients to Reach for a Word

they know, that comes to them like air
or the name of their first dog

or the children: *oldest, middle, baby*
though I am all my siblings now

the therapist says it's not unusual
for my mother to call her medicine *the virus*

as everything we've breathed this past year
is pandemic, normal for her to say she ate

the virus for breakfast lunch or dinner
—a side of virus, virus over-easy—

as every helper at the house is masked
but my mother remembers

scrambled soft, how my stepfather
held her close when she lost the job,

how he wore his one good suit
to deliver bad news but not the news itself

other than it concerned my grandmother
she remembers her husband loved

but my father hated. *My fault*, she says
of the divorce, enunciates *desire* quite clearly.

Riding Lessons

My father gave me horses. It's all he could do
to assuage the guilt of leaving us, though he had
no choice when my mother divorced him. First,
plastic replicas, a new model every birthday

or Christmas. The tawny palomino, the gray,
the buckskin I'd stand side by side on my shelf
where I could touch their cold plastic hides, imagine

hearts beating beneath. Then it was lessons: English,
with rules and a hefty price tag for my days
in the ring at a farm on the outskirts of town

where I learned form was everything
in all the gaits, though canter was in the wings
for us beginners. Walking, posting the trot, I found
my rhythm, cherished every ride,
but the only name I remember is Shiloh—

a bay I never rode, a gelding of many hands,
a battle of Union victory in the Civil War,
the turning point of someone's fate. I now know

Shiloh was also ancient river, Jewish sanctuary,
but at ten I didn't know the language of layers—
how one thing could mean many things
at once, like place or thing, or moving body,

a divide. I could only work my lesson horse—
shoulders back, heels down, hands low
on the reins, my legs squeezing signals for go
as I circled the ring in the sacred hour
that was all we had.

Everywhere We Once Knew Wildness

Past mounds of fuchsia azaleas,
raised rose beds, borders of purple-

spiked liriope, elephant ear, I race
through what's left of the neighborhood

we lived, will die in. Here, the oversized lot,
once thick with oaks. There, abodes

of embodied stability, sleepover—
dreams we could see in our neighbors'

sweeping routines, in faces
of parents hanging balloons

that would sway for weeks in trees
deflating. Through hawk's call, crow's caw

breeze past the home with overgrown shrubs
the owner will never tend

because her lover left, and between us, we all
have only so much to give back

to the ground, bending over and over
to unearth the dead, plant flats

full of any green hope
that might flower. From the jump

we knew here was where
we would settle, knew home

before sameness sank in. I round
a turn, return to crape myrtle, tea olive,

generations of bruised gardenias,
sprouted houses everywhere

we once knew wildness. Less is more,
we said, when we had nothing.

What's Left of Us Is Shaken

We know the drill: plywood cut to sills
to cover glass, bolted, battened down
to face the worst winds of a decade,
supercells spun inland from the sea.

Each hurricane worse than the last—
shock of debris, browned brush,
decapitated palms planted by a flock
of deniers. What's left of them,
of us, is shaken, wonders why rebuild?

We'll come back, it could have been worse.
Some of those blacked-out for days
made do with candlelight. Others discovered
how much brighter the stars appeared
in the darker nights.

What We Read About Ukraine Makes Us
Dream of Burning

On the road between villages
like Mriya and Myla, whose names mean Dream

and Sweetheart in our tongue,
mothers ink their children's backs

with family contacts: uncle, aunt, grandmother,
lest the mothers die and the children

be found alone. Lest we forget
the address they called home.

***

In my dream, I am a candle
that burned all night, despite the many ways
my wick might mushroom,

ignite. Like any good flame
I tapered, acquiescing
to my extinction.

Yet I wavered, just a little,
nestled in the candelabra's arm,
imagining a door might open,

and it would be you, holding an oil lamp
or a flashlight, moving toward me
just as close as you are far,

as if you never had the earth you came from torn
from your long fingers, stolen
like landscapes we took for granted

or the morning—you whose heart homed
like a pigeon, you my lost
light, language.

The Trees in Dealey Plaza Seemed Distressed

so county arborists trim live oaks on the knoll
where footsteps of a thousand tourists
over half a century compress soil

like buried memory. I was six, in first grade
curling cursive when Kennedy died
and my father arrived at the schoolyard

in our good used Ford, and said,
oh honey, shook his head.
I wish I could say I never looked back

but violence always cuts me down to size.
Some trees remember droughts, conserve
what water comes, a process of abscission,

building reservoir, a stand against
our misremembered dead.
Meanwhile, the arborists aim to reclaim

points of view, with each lopped limb,
strategic prune. Some retrace trajectory of bullet,
as if we could map regeneration, make old new.

Census

I cannot be without leaves / flying away and returning to earth.
—*Pablo Neruda*

Add a canopy of trees wind catapults
sky to field to forest—a blanket of the fallen—
to particles of ash from our pandemic dead.

Total our bits in a garden of remembrance,
a grand universe, an otherworld

we still embrace, an overarching *utopia*—
More's term, taking Greek for *not* and *place*
to arrive at a meadow the mind's eye envisions:

googols of lives, coming and going,
going, gone. Fragment and flesh, threshed

like grain from chaff. Auras
our beloveds wore, shimmering
to supermarket or cinema, or shed

for bed. Imagine a calculus of imprint, impact,
despite news of a star eating a planet

for the first time, sign of the sun's ultimate
consumption. Count on it, scientists say: Our burning end.
We look away. Imagine we soar like eagles,

born with hollow bones for flight.
I dream the dead reconstituted

as detritus—sacred meteors surpassing us
to shoot back vivid recollections
of a hundred billion galaxies, but let's get real:

even when we speak of infinites, we go below
the decimal of definition when we least expect

to be saved when something zenzic
in us rallies, rises—from and to
communities we'll lie and die with,

out of numbers, boundless, out of time.

Reverse Universe

The Gravitational Waves Would Like a Word

Turns out, a pull of zenzic yesterdays
vibrates everywhere in the garden

of agapanthus, unbeknownst to the starry violet blooms,
never more purple. The waves themselves

are colorless, reflect a fathomless violence
of astral events, yet we detect nary a shudder.

Who knew our dead parts could remain affixed
to our living, like phantom limbs

or the last generation? We thought we knew,
but it's proven now: our bodies are as close

as they are far. We spin, pretend
we're starting over. The waves whisper and shout.

**

Turns out, dead stars pulse ripples of space-time
light years wide. Background noise we try

to put aside comes crashing like regrets
of a billion suns postponed, then finally heard

in a new frequency. This time, pulsars
are star witnesses. Einstein saw it coming,

time expanded and compressed. Imagined a universal score.

**

Ahead of his time, King said the long arc
of the moral universe bends toward justice

but unimpeded by hope or despair, the waves just
propagate invisibly, shrink and stretch

all they touch. We wonder if it's still possible
to change the world, how to hold our little traumas.

Roll with it, we say.

**

We could be forgiven for a little hope
we'll one day see lost loves again,

our dolorifuge. You and I stopped dancing long ago,
no longer Nietzsche's roiled young souls

though he said something resonant
about eternal return. The gravitational waves

would like a word. Meanwhile, more supermassive
black holes undulate on someplace

before merging. Scientists celebrate
a symphony of cosmic notes. We try to follow,

fall back, hum a few bars.
The ripple effect. We laugh.

The ritual never gets old.

Reverse Universe

The fall shatters my right hand—
black speckling white metacarpals on the X-ray,

like a reverse universe. A splint, stop-gap
stability, allows my flesh to swell—
a river of purple tissue pushed to its banks

while I wait for the flood to subside—
bone repair takes time, cascades

of cytokines. I wave my arm
in the stockinette: a cast, a spell
of immobility. Astronomers say space expands,

contracts, but I'm content to move
what little ways I can, to spill the secrets

of my light years when my dying father asks me
how I'm doing, asks for coffee,
and I slide it from the Keurig with my good hand

fill the mug halfway with whole milk,
something stirred we have no words for.

Emergence

Inside my mother's belly, body
of the borrowed, I burrow

within a womb, congealed—
my *mise en abyme*, a story within
a story to follow

but I can't see to see. Sartre said
existence precedes essence, and it's true

we moved through broken water,
laboring a life—

a picture of desire and infinite regret
till, reading to the end, we sense

the props all fall, and cued,
what's left of us swims weightless back
through liquid day and night

to claim the moral,
mark our passages as one

as a hollow nesting doll emerges
from the matryoshka
in a child's delight.

In the Hollow

They say we imprint rhythms
of our parents' speech: what we knew
before we knew confinement,
what social distance meant.

In a cabin deep in Carolina woods,
my parents' voices ping like pennies
at the bottom of a well.
I believe we were content.

The last pandemic anyone remembered
predated us by generations.
I fall a little deeper into the echo chamber
of my mother's heartbeat.

Outside, nuthatch boxes hang
with the hope a threatened southern bird
will call them home.

A Purse Is a Mother Is My Birthright

I give her the feminine gender, this pride
on my sleeve, reflecting my taste.
Inside the gap of my scapula she hangs,

curved like a womb, a seamed strap wedding
her whole body—hip to shoulder—to mine,
taut at times, as when I press my hand

to the base of her sewn buckles, feel
my mother's fingers, still at the Singer,
hem-mending after fold and chalk.

Other times she bends into my side waist
muscles, as when I sit to listen as my mother
shares her latest skin flare-up, asks the specialist

to work her in, wonders if advancing years
will cause one's largest organ to grow thin,
or if that's just what physicians say

to help old women make peace with pain,
or when she leans against me for a moment,
lets me feel her weight. Bearing all I hold dear

zipped, she models merits of restraint,
yet elides a sigh from deep within her secret walls
when I reach down, across, inside her compartments

to claim my tube of lip gloss, lost keyrings,
forgotten change, a pair of shades, a buried pen
grit glistens. I emerge with all my broken bits

to see that everything we carry,
mold ourselves to, wears, fades away.
I think I don't deserve her, but I do.

Recovery

Police broke in when he didn't answer, found him cold, in rigor.
Some lividity, they said. After midnight when we got the call, he was
already at the morgue. Mother said he couldn't be embalmed,
should go to ground, post-haste. In his eighties, sick with flu that
week, when he didn't return her calls, she knew he'd stroked. She
wept and begged the medical examiner:

please, no autopsy—I swear he left us naturally—as we, his three
stepdaughters, drove from Tallahassee on Route 98 to the house
on Third Street, Mexico Beach, where he lived the sober quarter
of his life. Found his one good suit in the armoire, pressed—our
ghostly greeter—touched the fine grey wool one last time, conjured
how he'd dress for church, then shut the cabinet. Next, we hit
the kitchen, pitched the pound of ground chuck in the fridge.

Swiped his last spit from the sink, then made his bed, so Mother
wouldn't see the sweat-filled covers. We crumpled, set aside
the sheets he died in. Finishing, we fixed the broken lock, emptied
drawers of loose change, gathered all we found and loaded up
the truck—perhaps the only ones to see the gifts we'd given him,
hidden carefully, so neatly, in his chest.

The Great Egret

Pure white, all grace
note, still eye, plume,
bent yellow bill, drawn black leg—
a caught thought, a hiked skirt—

grazing this sea of asphalt,
one-time field, a fallow
cart-filled island fleetingly
in my rearview

like a fantasy of freedom
slammed to ground—

a sight to see, this great bird
claiming territory, scavenging
spilled groceries, crushed candy—
modesty be damned,

he'll take what he can get:
a naked truth, a gingered step

of whole intention, an imprinted act, flashback
to how we once found home,
our own true colors, white being

every hue of light.

Meanwhile, America Loses Its Memory

Absent his usual scribe, the chair
asks me to capture the long wind
of his council's diatribes. Pigeonholed,

I can't say no, so take my seat, and go
to work: note agenda items, consent first,
approved, then onto new business, the budget,

tranquil landscapes of our Florida springs
pending purchase for a building's hallways.
Discuss too much, too little saved,

discretionary extra for the best
selections, logistics of installation.
The unisex bathroom discussion stalls.

The cricket club's adviser raises the cost
of insurance, an issue all lament
as I condense their gists

to capture agreement or dissent.
A good year for the enterprise,
I type, should anyone review our balance—

how we paid our people for their days,
shorthanded what no record could convey.
Imagine what we know but cannot say.

After the Fall

No matter how far we've come,
our feet know the back way back
to the white frame house

in the historical register,
as if a building's record was our own,
as we relive significance of visits, calibrating

celebrations, deaths, what brings us
after all we know, back home.

Inside, the widow shares her plan—
caravan positions, who will lead and follow
to the church, fill pews in first.

Someone takes our cousin, the nonagenarian,
by the elbow, gently (*he is fine, thank you*)

leads him to the pebbles' grassy edge,
lined by violets, cabbage flower
purpling the portico's base

like a bruise. He places his father's cane,
a century-and-a-half old if a day,
sets the tip where purchase

may be gained—turns to us to affirm,
It was here, yes? Here he fell?

Knowing blood by sense, if not by sight,
how scrubbed steps still whisper to souls
with ears to landscaped rock—I say, *yes, Cousin.*

Cousin pauses, then tacks starboard,
like two brothers as young sailors did,
to stay a course, but sets this one alone,

winds the homestead's soft side path,
slowly as a clock.

Transitions: A Testimonial

Our father knows all five of us
and shows it—a hand, pressed. A nod

acknowledging each daughter here at last,
as animals seek shelter in the cold,
as however lost or found we feel

or felt, or will, we still seek home—
surviving selves in disembodied shells.

Chronos's hand sweeps across
the moment his kidneys fail. When blood flow
to the heart slows, stops—so

matter of fact. This is how we terrify
at symptoms from now on—each one
in light of layered diagnoses,

as we spot ourselves in the glass
of that sterile room and ask

what fate awaits us. On that day
we listen as the nurse says
hearing is the last to go, and cling to this

as we whisper our testimonies.

Relative Risk

No matter what the therapists say about dementia, how we
should know our half-blind mother can't live alone, how they are
clear she can't afford to fall—the only way to keep her going
on her own (not risk-free) is a scooter or a four-wheel walker, or to
move her to a place, they won't say where—best to keep
the care type vague—helpful doctors will tell you
recommended choices: memory pills, life locked inside, a safe
space, always a mask, no rugs or dancing, hugs, even
if your loved one, if Mom, is vaccinated, if
we instead allow her finger-walking walls, her wandering, it
wouldn't be the worst to drop and die at home, we'll say—what kills
is a voice silenced or a vision atrophied, when all your
good intention stymies dignity, what we recall of spirit.

The Attraction to Niagara

Some of them envied the Great Farini,
walking the tightrope, outdoing Blondin

with somersaults, headstands, hanging
by toes. Because to scale or jump

the short wire fence to float
to the falls' edge means brinkmanship

is close, or hope, at least, to lead the news—
imagine all those children

terrorized, clutching their parents, who look away.
It didn't have to end this way

they'll say, shaking their heads,
while stuck in the retina, a killer view of the gorge

marks another spectacular denouement,
a life surrendered to nature, or a final attempt

at ease. I remember the rush to judgment,
my eyes tracing the railing, no guards

on duty to protect this poor excuse
of a border—settled/wildness, life/death—

but whose job is it to keep another
from themselves? Are we not here

for the lore? Two to three a month go over,
the guide says, adding that against all odds,

a few of them have lived.

Tahané Recalls His Escape

An elderly gray wolf escaped from his northwest Florida preserve during
Hurricane Michael and was later found and returned to his owner.

Sixteen years, I feared no hunter, howled
for the crowd. My handler held my gentled heart,
controlled food, drink, and nearly all I knew
or needed to of life—raised captive, rarely growled,

no inkling of what lay beyond my gate.
Human acclimated, staff would say of my pack,
how we were never wild, yet modeled primal.
Nor was I an alpha, despite the myth, my fate

to have my day, my denouement, survive escape
and die of age, but that October, Michael hit,
the sky went black, wind shrieked, a great oak split
my fence, and I lunged into a broken landscape.

They said I fled of terror, but nature,
knowing what I couldn't, set me free.

Watching the Waning Gibbous Moon

shadow-boxing an afterlife
between full orb and new, its hidden opposite,

we move, as if pulled out to sea,
into transition's blur. Discern

familiar flaws, our own resistance
cycling in and out of view,

like old scars, faint-cratered
topography. Years feel like days

eclipsed as we arc and hide,
hold fast like stars through mutual gravity.

The moon is dead, you said
last summer in Moab, guessing

when the sun would set, using fingers
for each hour. I tried my hand,

and I'm still trying, as Polaris
points true north, as we vanish

like volcanoes, dead a billion years.
I'm convinced I'll find myself

if lost, be seen by some
as whole, so not a fear worth keeping

if you believe we've passed the stage of stellar
evolution when we all burn out

or if we learn to live, as Atlas did, with the heavens,
holding each other, the world.

Evidence

Daylight Savings

In the lidded hour, in the usual dark,
I rise to imagine the moon
alongside still-visible stars.

Outside my downward slanted blinds,
night sounds: barred owl, cricket, peeper.
Just a few more minutes, I tell God

as if praying names of the dead
might spring their lost time forward,
those who weathered midwestern winters,

blood zeroed out—my grandfather, for one,
who stroked and died at sixty-seven
though he lived to hold me,

his tiny Indiana visitor at three, too early
or too late for snow. All he did by then was smile,
unaware of who would carry on

or how hard the years to come
would be beyond the longest days,
lives collapsed between the present and the past

the way my father came to crave
his stinkbug South, its musk and dusk
before his time ran out

the season changed,
and our lives, like an hourglass
turned over.

Fault Line
(for SSM)

The phrase never tells the whole story—so much more
than surface, length, or two rocks sliding past
each other, fractured Earth. Planetary mother,
prism bending light, I fell between your faults

my face refracting the quiet street you'd moved to,
newly married, sparkling in our first house.
Where we stayed after Father moved out. Forgiveness
isn't free, or linear, even the point—

nor my marled memory, oft rehashed:
righteous, always so righteous, you screamed after the affair,
when a chair or an object was thrown in the room
you and my father shared, my ear at the door, guessing.

Orphaned now, I quake, I orbit you as I did as a child,
dog-bitten, bitter, burned by a boy. Flash my scar.

The Landing

Before we took our turns to jump,
we saw the butterfly's burned body splayed
across a boulder, eyespots split,

ellipses dragging on and over
what was left of chest or head.

No telling how long it was dead.
Sixty years later, I still remember
its blue-black blood, that blend

of iridescence and death, the shock:
Strange boys, feet in the rocky river

below us, their low laughs. Side-eye,
a secret. We couldn't call them killers

back then—didn't witness the deed—
yet now I know we knew. The fire was gone,

the matches' spark, but the bruise flew,
alit on my dissolving heart
or the part of my mind once capable

of forgiveness. A purpling testament.
Scant hope grown dark.

Geography

Do you remember when we understood
our place on Earth? We moved,

at home with ourselves,
children of our own incessant growth,

seeking our mothers in each other,
or any good microclimate of warmth.

Love, listen: before sunscreen,
I absorbed every ultraviolet ray,

no fear of freckle or burn, until one day,
poolside in my black bikini,

I dozed off as the sun beat into me
pigment isn't permanent—

some stars we feel as friends can turn on us.
After the peel, the sloughing off

of damaged cells revealed Florida
on my chest: a spotted peninsula

for curiosity seekers to finger-walk
highways, back roads, a stop to linger

at the Circle K, to trace a path to glistening
Panhandle beaches, blister—

what we see, or think we see,
this world one endless bubble of light.

My breath falls, rises with the sea.
Some tourists visiting my landmarks stayed,

sailed with me, some veered off course.
One took a side trip to the big cat reserve

for the keeper-of-the-day experience. They were
game but gone too soon on other expeditions.

I looked into celestial navigation
to evaluate my cosmic relativity,

searched on land, at sea for bearing.
Dropped anchor occasionally

but in my present state, I turn again,
with all my scars, Icarian,

to face the sun,
my wrong cartography.

Look: you're here; I'm here, I say
to my flawed body,

listening for a guide.
You should know, whoever you are

in whatever hurricane bar or Denny's
you wind up in, you are home.

You Can Stay in a Place Too Long

Even our homes tire of us—
the once-bold area rugs,
red madder root patterns bleeding

from light they lay in
year after year, tread upon and admired
in equal measure. Dirt ground into tile

seals secrets like kisses, like passion
flowers in the overgrown yard
we debrided, suturing

to heal a landscape when our hands
flew in and out of pots,
when no heat could make us stop,

until we cooled, forgot. Frayed edges
fill familiar rooms—
in each corner, a context

begs forgiveness, justifies
the ways we dug into our digs
before the walls closed in

and off, like power
flipped. We weren't at fault for wanting
domiciles in which to hide, to live

or die, make work our life,
make love to last forever.
We were blips. We know this now.

Evidence

Her last night as a breathing
entity, my mother skirrs into sky
like a flock of seabirds startled from shellfish by dog

signs of distress, they said, but we weren't there
to testify, instead, imagine this:

A lift of wings, of wheeling gulls,
and there's that ship we read of in the poem,
leaving shore—a spread of white sails

shrinking into the blue pelagic
as another vision greets the vessel warmly

from the other side, beyond what anyone who waved goodbye
could see, or hear in the sea's sough
but when my feet find sand—sand soft enough

to sink in at high tide this bitter morning after
a record freeze, I level up, keep going, watch

my step, then spot a cloven hoof—no, four, no, eight, no—
even more upside-down hearts
tracking north, a running herd of deer

below a crescent moon or breaking dawn—
a sprint from a known preserve

to a protected park, we speculate,
across the towered condos, gated surfside
neighborhoods, past gutted dunes, depressed

amidst the human prints, dog paw
impressions—something urgent, something new

to follow, wait for. Believe in.
Something wild.

The Beach House Offers an Elegy

My owners opened me to strangers
all my life. I house snowbirds, impress

weekenders, retirees, turn myself
inside out, season after season, summer

into fall, upgrade my scaffolding
and wall to wall, refine the touches

one expects to please, but the bones
of my existence bear your own

indelibly. I indulge my tenants' hunger—
longing is my raison d'être. All this time,

I've held your breath—praise you gave
the view from the boardwalk,

emptiness you may have expressed,
unwound for a week's vacation—

I exhale you from this space:
at one level, how you were known.

The sun you watched rise over the dunes
from the patio sets, resets. Diabetic shoes you wore

when feeling left your feet left no mark
on the porcelain tile, which to this day

appreciates forgiveness: give and take,
the net sum of our wanderings.

Let me say the guest book loved your leafing,
reading what others had left.

The closet that sheltered your few simple shirts
wishes everyone could be so easy

to protect. Memory foam in the queen
mattress made unusual accommodation

of your long, heavy body. Comfort layers
in the plush endure, depressed.

The bedside lamp you read beside until midnight
burns for you tonight. When you moved from earth

to dust or starlight—if it matters—
fronds from a silk palm in the bedroom

brushed another lover's shoulder passing
in the night. They would tell you touch

remembers touch. No one knows the ways
we let each other go.

All My Father's Heroes

seemed less holy when we found them
stacked in storage, long removed
from walls where, hung strategically
above my father's desk, they called

his name in study after study,
in each house he'd live without us—

Schweitzer, Tillich, King, portrait saints
who relished their indwelling,
though we'd claim space too,
in smaller frames, and we've come down

with death as well. We are not
the only ones left lesser, fending—

not because we couldn't be great men
or women, when the world saw us
as children—not because the animals
our heroes loved can't speak

of whom they dutifully obeyed
or of a certain tenderness

familiar hands conveyed in sweet caress
or steepled, knowing all
or nothing, bent in prayer—
but because when what we worship dies

or falls from grace, what's lost
ransoms our innocence; we're left

an empty slate. If memory were coin
we'd pay our savings, piece by piece,
redeem each unseen face.

The Old Loblolly Shares Your Future and Your Past

When you palm my darkening scales
I break for you, who always eyed your mother

at the screen door, feet away
from where I stood, a sentry—
where each day love opened to let you in.

Not that you didn't know me:
bulwark, pillar pine behind the stately live oaks

with their clustered leaves, their acorn scatter
coexisting, where you couldn't see me
peering down from sixty feet

or reaching for stars, although I'm used to being overlooked.
As you pull me from myself

my bark falls through your fingers,
furrowed benisons of shelter, shade you took

for granted, though it was my job
to fade. Before the house sells and you leave me

one last time, spread your fingers, watch my shatter fall
to the ground, remember fizzle-pop of leaf
at night, how rain broke through my canopy

and was heard to comfort, in the home within the walls
once so alive with sound.

Because We Can't Remember Doesn't Mean It Didn't Happen

The night she died, the sky was clear
and full of stars, above the outer edges

of her old live oaks, loblolly, stark relief
against the blackness, absence

of mist. A silence into which time fell,
hours past or before the gloaming.

 I strained hard to see beyond the lacy veil of leaves
for any trace of memory

of when she, too, might have ventured out
at dark into this yard she'd known and tended

over forty-five years, and gazed up
at a starry field, if only to be dazzled

by the open clusters, windows into space
unknown and felt if only briefly

Hera, Milky Way split from her breast,
and seen her children waiting, or not far behind

in mysteries of the finite world, infinite time,
and smiled, at peace, then went inside

and cut the light to sleep.
I came up blank.

Hours later, the call came. No one could tell us
if she was alone.

When Time Ran Out, I Took the Clock In

Where black-arrowed hands ticked
predictably for years, a house's beating heart,

a still, round space. Its yellow face
had faded, like our tourbillon of hope
against life's gravity, within the silenced chimes—

no wing, no prayer, a generation, or a few,
passing in seconds. We'd long since
stopped holding time like a hostage between us,

ransoming the old betrayals—
all we counted on to kill that elephant of remembrance

to which we finally succumb
as silence fills my mother's living room
like a pitcher full of need,

empty of tea. In my greed
to set things right, I took the clock in.

Sorry for bad news, horologists said—
vintage parts are hard to find
and labor lags for restoration. Gave a price

that blew my mind, then offered up
that it was fine to love it dead.

I placed the slate-cased clock up high
enough to lift my eyes,
like a child to imagined angels.

If the Fragment is the Story

then the letter Arnold sent my mother in the '80s
was nothing more, nothing less than his script

on letterhead, reminding her of their bond
as classmates at Miami High, where once

is always, everyone heeds each other, melting
in time, and along those lines, he has friends in high places—

a certain Senator if you want to know—
who'd be happy to help her find work

if she needs it, before, in closing, Arnold says
whenever he thinks of girls from back then,

it is she who comes to mind
as the sweetest—one he has never forgotten—

but there is no blatant invitation, never does he say
he's married, ask if she's happy or how many children

and when I look for traces of him
elsewhere in her hope chest, he is nowhere

in her yearbooks; not a single note from him
appears alongside other scrawled *goodbyes, good lucks*

nor is he listed with the smiling others
in the photo of the kindergarten play,

no clipped obituary, evidence of her reply
but on the jagged edge of a leaf torn from an album,

I imagine Arnold there professed his love
before a jealous ex wiped clean my mother's memory

for suitors, her nostalgia for pure desire—
left Arnold unfulfilled and buried in the cedar

with our baby clothes, in the margins,
holding secrets we were never meant to know.

Speaking of God

On an island full of slash pine and palmetto,
crows staccato-warn of us in the canopy

as my dog relieves himself and I slacken our leash
while his stream interrogates the shepherd's needle
as we face the hoped-for promise of another day

along with the early purple blooms
of our agapanthus, bearing their umbel inflorescence,
though climate confused. I, too, feel out of season

beneath the red-barred breast of a low-flying hawk,
light, above all, light, imprinted
in my every nerve, umbrella

shielding what I dream yet cannot see. Old friend,
I still seek signs of you in any green thing

growing, any clue that you might see me,
nestled in this life, as the greater sandhills migrate
to another state, as I breathe in pollen,

your miraculous dust. See me shining, half-lit,
from the third-eye pineal view—
waking, winded, how I burn for you.

Survival Guide

Lacuna

Great-aunt Nina's tiny souvenirs
from Europe, tucked in tissue
in a cardboard box a niece would find
generations from her person,
transferred home to home—

dreams of Paris, Rome, as far away
or close as touch. Our mother's life
in scrapbooks bagged and tied, in white ink
on black paper, captioning her birth, first ocean

swim, tea party. Look—they toast the baby
while the Great Depression rages, just as Nero
fiddled while Rome burned, while we
flip aging pages, all they hold still perfectly intact

as if we could gather an inkling
of her origins and take it home,
bind her early life to later to our own

as if we could learn from letters she kept
ribboned in a folder, all she never told us—
trauma, separation, therapy, her diary,
two husbands, hopes for reconciliation honed.
We know what happens next,

how open endings close. When movers come for the armoire
and her low-boy chest, I palm the brass pulls
one last time, breathe emptiness—

a lacuna where we'd found Aunt Nina's sterling
folded in a secret drawer, a spot we nearly missed,
by the divider separating silver dollars, underwear,
the cat's old collar, ankle socks and sleep shirts

gone to thrift stores when our mother left
for good, bequeathing all she couldn't take
and wouldn't now recall.

All You Can Fit in A Suitcase

Three tanks, an all-weather sweater
for layering, thermals. Leggings, a pair

of well-treaded boots for forced marching
in this hypothetical, which imports me

into your country like an unwanted pest,
or an exotic species.

In the sides, tuck rhinestone toe-posts—
for sparkle, like champagne, like leisure-to-go—

or my mother's diamond solitaire
with the story of my father's postal route that bought it

and the grief they carried
when the bloom fell off the rose

sewn into a parka pocket. There'll be room left
for my native birdsong on a flash drive,

notecards with embossed gold leopards
right below the fold, as from the depths

of territory I can't bring myself to navigate,
I'll pen what's left of my salvation

in the lining, like a legend you can follow
mapping how caged hopes burst free

like the restless wild cat dimmed
in memory, a handy guide to hold the world

in hand like the bird you know
and the heart you can't,

closer to the vest than any secret.

Last of the Honeyeaters

The 'ō'ō' bird was endemic to the island of Kauai.

Scientists who listen for a living
logged my hollow dirge
from the montane forests to the canyons
where we could no longer nest

nonetheless we numbered thirty-four
in the 1960s, but Iwa and Iniki
took our oldest trees, what was left
of our essential cavities.

**

Two of us lived in the stream valleys
in '81, a pair. But she went first, and I
was soon to follow. I sang a song
like tolling bells, some said, commenting

how my sorrow reshaped air.
In truth, I gave it all to lust
before I gasped my last.

**

Hear me now, online, remixed,
my zenzic, amplified despair,
as if the world had never changed
my lip of joy to lament.

Close your eyes, escape. Imagine me
in all my black-and-golden-feathered glory—
plucked in molt by birdmen
for a king's cape—

and if you need a hook to hang a hope on,
tell yourself I'm never really gone.

Intimates

We were told to label our mother's clothes
to reduce the risk of loss

so all the pieces I retrieved
when she died are marked in permanent ink

as if her smell was not enough to testify
she lived. Nothing fit me but a pair of panties

so I wash and wear her branded intimates
because she taught us to repurpose or reuse.

I think she would approve: her garment
on my body, which from birth she watched

take shape—a familiar resting place
for one small thing she needed that we saved

though she'd say her name on the backside
made her feel like an inmate.

So much more of me than she
hangs over the band

that covered her soft-as-cotton skin
so thin at the end, so fair—

one who never sought the sun,
although she grew up in the Gables,

Coconut Grove. I've never burned
the way I burned in Miami,

facing an emerald ocean, flat on my back
for hours after scattering her ashes.

Dress Code

After the first season of grief
I rearranged my life in layers—
staggered separates, flash of color,

simple dolorifuge. First, I stopped buying blouses
with buttons, shoes with straps
for years I bent to fasten, heels

I towered in to tell myself, no matter what
I'd rise above, moved to flats
and open toes. In summer, I clung

to my sheath, vest-
ed in sweat, absorbed my body's tears
until they dried on the underside. Sleeveless

was freeing when I'd flail.
In autumn, I added a shrug.

***

Some noticed my abandon,
called it *simply age*, as if loss

had reached my head, as if I could skirt
apologies, regret. Others knew rules
were meant to be broken, like timelines,

like hemlines—waterfall, they call them now—
rise and fall, the way we mourn our dead.

Grief becomes me, I think.
Rest in sadness, one said,

seeing shape in my madness,
due process in my billowing black dress.

***

When the new year rolled around
too soon for changing, I stripped down—

broke the code of costume
in my dark room in my skin of origin,

loosed whatever look and feel
I thought would save me, savoring for once

the body my mother once dressed, undressed.

Pendulum

Our first house had floor-to-ceiling windows
allowing all the light, and the lake view—

a ribbon stretched wildlife to wetlands,
cottonmouths twisted in cypress knees
on islands we kayaked between

when the lake reached record highs
and we followed each other over and under

like a Möbius strip. I can't tell you when
we lost track of time or our place in it—

Was it when we saw a gator
plow the water with intent,
knew we could no longer swim

or play dummy fetch with the dog
at the shore where wild turkeys foraged

in leaf litter, and knew as well, despite
the rumor, they would fly and roost
in trees nearby? Was that when we snapped?

I remember the leave I took
when you weren't looking, the reeling in
of a dead reptile by those we called our friends.

We'd set the trap and fallen for it, but the stories
blend—a time span, water's weight, the depression

we buried the dog in—still hold sway.
The fairytale we believed, return to,

still displaced. The ways we let each other go.

The Bell

Just like that, it's summer.
All the deciduous trees stop shedding

before we even notice the driveway's
pure concrete, empty of leaf debris

or understood we'd not been blowing
for weeks. The robin's song

at dawn as clear as the jangle
of the red jingle bell, a ball

at the bottom of the beaded string
my mother wore each Christmas,

now ringing the rearview mirror
in my SUV, where each morning I start the engine,

roar to work, but not before
I remember her sparkling

prior to the last season's pallor.
I shake the body of tiny beads

as if her bones could tintinnabulate
until the trembling stills in my palm

between the heart and lifelines
and the bell rests, finally subdued.

Hunger

Bags of safflower, millet seed
from the wild bird store build bones
of tufted titmice, Carolina wren,

kernel by nut by chip at the feeder,
if you believe the flyer
flexing nutrients. Finches cling

to the shroud, while others hover
like storm clouds over the pole, dive deep
or dissipate, like the last thought you thought

to collect. We almost can't trust
what we see anymore, or read,
our vision fading, chasing sun

or is it radiance, a scarlet cardinal in the bush?
Those who linger at the tray's lip poke
in/out of ports, like little lasers,

titmice flash orange-tinted breasts
at the baffle's edge. A chickadee tips
its black cap as I finger the focusing thumbwheel

of my binoculars, perched on my kitchen chair
at twilight, as if I were magnet
to hunger, witness to a fleeting common cause

amidst a diaspora, displacement certain
in development to come. Imagine a diapason
outside my back porch, all the birds drawn

to a shredded kernel. Retina of memory.
Any heart at all.

Viral

1

Something akin to memory reactivated
sparks my skin to burn within

and I lose touch with touch.
Inspect me, I say, after shedding shirt, bra,
bent over our bed.

You lean toward my back,
seeking blisters like burns,
like too much sun leaves,

or how we feel when we believe ourselves
infallible, my rash, or what's left

of my last indecisions,
proof of my hem and haw:

treat nerve pain with gabapentin
or lidocaine? How much of everything
am I allowed?

I throw down the pills and patches,
like a gauntlet: *Come for me.*

Meanwhile, you scan what I can't see.
Even the sheets hurt, I say.

2

Helvetesild, Norwegians call it—
hell's fire, around my dermatome:

shingles, from the Latin *cingulum,* meaning belt,
called *zoster* by the ancient Greeks, for girdle.
Robin Williams had it. As did Richard Nixon

and Roseanne. Your mother, my father, me—
the ones-in-three this virus will awaken in,

like a volcano venting, or an earthquake—
a bodily event no fault evokes,
latent in the dorsal root ganglia.

We spoke of roots the other week,
compared migrations on the ancestry website.
Your people would never spit in a vial,

send DNA to a company, you said,
like so much cash or social currency,

as if genetic code might trace propensities,
or immunity from pestilence.

What you don't know can't hurt you,
Father used to say when I was young,
and he knew everything.

Socrates said the only true wisdom
is in knowing you know nothing.

I know nothing but my body's secrets,
which I'll keep for life.

3

You can't catch it from me, I say
as you shift me from my shoulders—this way, that—
like the earth spins around its axis,

and I'm suddenly sun or moon,
your permanent satellite, beaming evidence:

angry red grows dull around my torso,
or my color changes, like a chameleon

as you move me side to side,
your eyes a log of all my body holds.

In the Balance of the Years Between Us

At his age, I was dreaming horses,
rocking in my father's lap—

> *This is the way the ladies ride,*
> *trit trot, trit trot*

—my father would sing, slow at first, then up the clip
as gentlemen rode, then cowboys, then cowgirls—

> *giddy-up, giddy-up, whoa!*

I'd squeal.

The rhyme comes back to me
when I gaze down to my toes

between the hands I hold
into my grandson's smile, his toddler teeth,

his breeze-tossed hair. He buckles his knees
then laughs, towheaded hope,

his feet raised high to swing.
I let him sway   I push   he kicks the air

tantivy of a new generation rising
like warming seas, inundating a landscape of loss

but my grandson bounces, begs his legs
to fly. In the balance of the years between us,

I hear voices, tinned like ghosts,
or if I listen close, a whinny.

Refuge

Sixty-seven species nest on the Bear River refuge—
American avocets, black-necked stilts

by the thousands spike dikes and roads
we wind on our way back

to the hotel, wilted from dry heat, wetlands,
imagine bird calls heard/

unheard from across a wilderness of seen/
unseen migrations, droughts—

a land of shrinking lakes to which they all return,
nestlings and the species left

alone to fend against the wildfires
of a burning age. Though we missed the tundra

swans this trip, a small regret,
we tell ourselves our mothers did their jobs

for here we are, a nested pair,
flown decades married through the motions

of layovers, stops and starts, our settled life
to which we turn and turn again,

despite imprinted restlessness, free-falling
as the great Salt Lake evaporates.

The Chickadees Are All Up in Our Feelings

We watched them grab and go,
gripping the suet with tiny black feet,
then skirring sky, a blur of rolling wing,
then back to perch to chisel meat from hull—

tried not to take their brisk appearance
personally, so proud were we to see
the fruit of all our baffling
rewarded with black caps and bibs

of birds we'd never known
lived in our trees: Carolina chickadees,
layering the forest canopy like ghosts,
caching seed or scavenged bits of dead

their memories imprint, along with space
and time, and all the lost, the stolen.
So focused were we on our own recovery,
we never sensed them scatter-hoarding

under fallen leaves, knotholes—
even our old asphalt shingles
shadow their tuck and hide, we gather
from the guidebook, glued to our seats

on the porch, where we glass
their bandit masks, as a family pokes,
prods for feed. Scientists say
a larger hippocampus serves the species well

in the season of remembering,
when stored cells grow and die,
replenishing through winter's hunger,
when the chickadees return to flit and fly
to every buried need.

Survival Guide

The wolf never came to the door,
though we imagined it howling.
Somehow the lights stayed on.
The chuck-will's-widow's whistle vanished
from summer nights, yet still we listen at dusk
and dawn for the owls' duet—hoot, cackle, caw—

wake to imprinted cardinal, mourning dove,
but also birdsong we can't name,
mysterious as the universe we'll never fathom,
having relinquished the ghost of knowing

to constellations we'll never see, to voices dreamed
but never heard, or heard no more—
yet, too, that haunting cry, airglow,
the occasional river of stars.

ACKNOWLEDGMENTS

Some of the poems listed below appeared in earlier versions in the following publications. I am deeply grateful to the editors of these journals for their support.

Atlanta Review: "The Chickadees Are All Up in Our Feelings" and "Proof"
Asheville Review: "Flyover"
ASP Bulletin: "The Trees in Dealey Plaza Seemed Distressed"
Bear River Review: "The Grief Committee"
Broad River Review: "Meanwhile, America Loses Its Memory"
Cumberland River Review: "Emergence"
Five Points: "The Great Egret"
Florida Review: "Relative Risk"
Gulf Coast: "What We Read About Ukraine Makes Us Dream of Burning"
Grist: "Recovery"
Kestrel: "Evidence"
Louisiana Literature: "Riding Lessons" and "Avian Inventory"
One Art: "All You Can Fit in a Suitcase"
Pacifica: "Intimates"
River Heron Review: "If the Fragment is the Story"
Rust and Moth: "You Can Stay In A Place Too Long"
Redivider: "It's Common for Alzheimer's Patients to Reach for a Word"
San Pedro River Review: "Fault Line"
South Dakota Review: "Pendulum"
Split Rock Review: "What's Left Of Us Is Shaken" and "The Attraction to Niagara"
Stirring: "Geography"
Sugar House Review: "Refuge"
Sweet: A Literary Confection: "In the Hollow," "Survival Guide," and "Tahané Recalls His Escape"
SWWIM Every Day: "A Pileated Woodpecker Shares Where to Find God," "A Purse Is My Mother Is My Birthright," and "Transitions: A Testimonial"
Trampset: "When Time Ran Out, I Took the Clock In"

Twelve Mile Review: "The Brazilian Peppertrees" and "Daylight Savings"

UCity Review: "After the Fall," "Speaking of God," "Reverse Universe," and "Viral"

Valparaiso Poetry Review: "Lacuna"

Whale Road Review: "The Beach House Offers an Elegy"

Worcester Review: "All My Father's Heroes"

Yemassee: "Watching the Waning Gibbous Moon"

Zone 3: "Space Invaders" and "Everywhere We Once Knew Wildness"

Some work in this book received additional recognition, for which I am both humbled and appreciative.

"The Trees in Dealey Plaza Seemed Distressed" won third place in the Alan Squire Publishing Bulletin's first annual poetry contest in 2023 and was also a semifinalist for the 2023 James Applewhite Poetry Prize sponsored by the *North Carolina Literary Review.*

"Proof" was a finalist in the *Atlanta Review's* 2023 International Poetry Contest.

"If the Fragment is the Story" was a finalist in the 2022 *River Heron Review* Poetry Contest. "Survival Guide" was a finalist in *Sweet: A Literary Confection's* 2022 poetry contest.

"Meanwhile, America Loses its Memory" was a finalist for the 2019 Rash Award sponsored by *Broad River Review.*

Whale Road Review nominated "The Beach House Offers an Elegy" for a Pushcart Prize in 2021.

"A Pileated Woodpecker Shares Where to Find God" appeared in *Rewilding: Poems for the Environment,* an anthology published by Flexible Press in 2020, and in *Chameleon Chimera, An Anthology of Florida Poets,* published by Purple Ink Press, in 2024.

SWWIM Every Day nominated "A Pileated Woodpecker Shares Where to Find God" for the Orison Anthology in 2019 and awarded third place to "A Purse Is My Mother Is My Birthright" in the journal's "Purses for Poetry" contest that year.

Split Rock Review nominated "What's Left of Us is Shaken" for a Pushcart Prize in 2019.

UCity Review selected me as its "Noteworthy Poet" in Issue 21/2020 and published several of the poems that appear in this book.

The manuscript that became this book was a finalist for the Marsh Hawk Press Poetry Prize, the Barry Spacks Poetry Prize and the Wandering Aengus Book Award.

Endless thanks to my husband, Chad, for his ongoing support as patience. April Ossmann, Erica Wright and Martha Silano all provided valuable editorial feedback and helped me shape the book into its present form.

I'm grateful to my family, friends and co-workers who have followed my writing journey and encouraged me at every stage of it, offering encouragement and validation when I've most needed it. To Saint Julian Press and Ron Starbuck, enormous gratitude for bringing this work into the world.

NOTES

Linda Pastan's poem, "List," appeared in *Poetry* (The Poetry Foundation, 1982)

"Relative Risk" is a Golden Shovel variation after Katie Englehart's opinion piece, "We Are Going to Keep You Safe Even if It Kills Your Spirit," published in *The New York Times* (Feb. 19, 2021)

Thomas Altizer, whose name appears in "A Pileated Woodpecker Shares Where to Find God," was a university professor, religion scholar and theologian who became the face of the "Death of God" movement in the 1960s and 1970s.

Paul Tillich's quote in "Proof" is from *The Courage to Be* (Yale University Press, 1952)

Pablo Neruda's quote in "Census" appeared in his poem "I Ask for Silence," from *Extravagaria*, (Losada, 1958)

ABOUT THE AUTHOR

Sarah Carey is a North Carolina native who grew up in Florida and has spent most of her life there. She attended Duke University and Florida State University, where she received a master's degree in English with a creative writing concentration. Her work has appeared in numerous journals, including *Gulf Coast, Five Points, Rattle, Florida Review, Atlanta Review,* and elsewhere. Sarah is the author of two poetry chapbooks, including *Accommodations*, winner of the 2018 Concrete Wolf Chapbook Award, (Concrete Wolf Poetry Series, 2019) and *The Heart Contracts*, (Finishing Line Press, 2016.) She has worked in journalism and public relations for her entire professional career, including over 30 years as director of communications for the University of Florida College of Veterinary Medicine, and has amassed numerous honors and awards for her writing. She lives in Gainesville with her husband and a big black Lab.

Visit her Amazon author page to learn more about Sarah and order her books.

https://amazon.com/author/sarahcarey

Her website is: https://sarahkcarey.com/.

You can also find her on Facebook @SarahKCarey, on Twitter/X @SayCarey1 and on Instagram @skcarey1.

www.ingramcontent.com/pod-product-compliance
Lightning Source LLC
Chambersburg PA
CBHW071205120626
46546CB00006B/2431